To: _____

From: _____

Family Recipes to Share

WELCOME!

With this one-of-a-kind recipe book, you can share your culinary expertise with your family while creating a treasured keepsake. Fill it with your favorite recipes, memories, advice, and love to build an invaluable cooking guide in the kitchen. Whether it's for a special occasion or just to show you care, this gift will be an irreplaceable heirloom that will be cherished for years to come.

HOW TO USE THIS RECIPE KEEPER

As you fill in the Advice section of this book, think of your own first days in the kitchen. Here you can place helpful tips, useful substitutions, table etiquette, memorable moments, and inspiration that will encourage your loved ones to try new recipes and pass them on to their own families.

The recipe keeper is divided into eight tabbed sections. The beginning of each section has a page set aside for your notes, ideas, or family photos. You can also include magazine and newspaper cutouts, copies of recipes from favorite cookbooks, stickers, or photos of food to embellish the book.

The following recipe pages have a place for the recipe title, your name, and the amount of people the recipe serves. You can handwrite the recipe, paste a typed version onto the page, or include a handwritten recipe from a family member or friend — remember, the design of the book is up to you! Each section also has a recipe index for easy reference, providing a place to record recipe names, where the recipes are from, and page numbers.

We hope this special keepsake brings much joy and many delicious meals to your loved ones. Above all else, it is a gift from the heart and a beautiful expression of the love and devotion you feel for your family. Enjoy!

Advice from My Kitchen

HELPFUL COOKING TIPS I KNOW

_____
_____
_____
_____
_____
_____
_____
_____
_____
_____
_____
_____
_____
_____
_____
_____
_____
_____

CREATED BY: _____

DATE: _____

Appetizers

Notes

RECIPE _____

FROM THE KITCHEN OF _____

SERVES _____

_____
_____
_____
_____
_____
_____
_____
_____
_____
_____
_____
_____
_____
_____
_____
_____
_____
_____
_____
_____
_____
_____
_____
_____
_____

RECIPE _____

FROM THE KITCHEN OF _____

SERVES _____

RECIPE _____

FROM THE KITCHEN OF _____

SERVES _____

_____

_____

_____

_____

_____

_____

_____

_____

_____

_____

_____

_____

_____

_____

_____

_____

_____

_____

_____

_____

_____

_____

RECIPE _____

FROM THE KITCHEN OF _____

SERVES _____

_____
_____
_____
_____
_____
_____
_____
_____
_____
_____
_____
_____
_____
_____
_____
_____
_____
_____
_____
_____
_____
_____
_____
_____
_____
_____
_____

RECIPE _____

FROM THE KITCHEN OF _____

SERVES _____

_____
_____
_____
_____
_____
_____
_____
_____
_____
_____
_____
_____
_____
_____
_____
_____
_____
_____
_____
_____
_____
_____
_____
_____
_____

RECIPE _____

FROM THE KITCHEN OF _____

SERVES _____

_____
_____
_____
_____
_____
_____
_____
_____
_____
_____
_____
_____
_____
_____
_____
_____
_____
_____
_____
_____
_____
_____

RECIPE _____

FROM THE KITCHEN OF _____

SERVES _____

RECIPE _____

FROM THE KITCHEN OF _____

SERVES _____

_____
_____
_____
_____
_____
_____
_____
_____
_____
_____
_____
_____
_____
_____
_____
_____
_____
_____
_____
_____
_____
_____
_____
_____
_____

RECIPE _____

FROM THE KITCHEN OF _____

SERVES _____

_____
_____
_____
_____
_____
_____
_____
_____
_____
_____
_____
_____
_____
_____
_____
_____
_____
_____
_____
_____
_____
_____
_____
_____

RECIPE _____

FROM THE KITCHEN OF _____

                                    SERVES _____

_____

_____

_____

_____

_____

_____

_____

_____

_____

_____

_____

_____

_____

_____

_____

_____

_____

_____

_____

_____

_____

_____

_____

RECIPE _____

FROM THE KITCHEN OF _____

SERVES _____

_____
_____
_____
_____
_____
_____
_____
_____
_____
_____
_____
_____
_____
_____
_____
_____
_____
_____
_____
_____
_____
_____
_____

RECIPE _____

FROM THE KITCHEN OF _____

SERVES _____

_____
_____
_____
_____
_____
_____
_____
_____
_____
_____
_____
_____
_____
_____
_____
_____
_____
_____
_____
_____
_____
_____

RECIPE _____

FROM THE KITCHEN OF _____

SERVES _____

_____
_____
_____
_____
_____
_____
_____
_____
_____
_____
_____
_____
_____
_____
_____
_____
_____
_____
_____
_____
_____
_____
_____
_____

RECIPE _____

FROM THE KITCHEN OF _____

                                    SERVES _____

_____
_____
_____
_____
_____
_____
_____
_____
_____
_____
_____
_____
_____
_____
_____
_____
_____
_____
_____
_____
_____
_____
_____

RECIPE _____

FROM THE KITCHEN OF _____

SERVES _____

_____
_____
_____
_____
_____
_____
_____
_____
_____
_____
_____
_____
_____
_____
_____
_____
_____
_____
_____
_____
_____
_____
_____
_____

RECIPE _____

FROM THE KITCHEN OF _____

SERVES _____

_____
_____
_____
_____
_____
_____
_____
_____
_____
_____
_____
_____
_____
_____
_____
_____
_____
_____
_____
_____
_____
_____

RECIPE _____

FROM THE KITCHEN OF _____

SERVES _____

_____
_____
_____
_____
_____
_____
_____
_____
_____
_____
_____
_____
_____
_____
_____
_____
_____
_____
_____
_____
_____
_____

RECIPE _____

FROM THE KITCHEN OF _____

SERVES _____

_____
_____
_____
_____
_____
_____
_____
_____
_____
_____
_____
_____
_____
_____
_____
_____
_____
_____
_____
_____
_____
_____
_____
_____

More Recipes to Love

Use this page to organize additional recipes you want to include
in this section. List the recipe's title, source, and page number.

RECIPE TITLE	SOURCE	PAGE NUMBER

Brunch Dishes

Notes

RECIPE _____

FROM THE KITCHEN OF _____

SERVES _____

_____

_____

_____

_____

_____

_____

_____

_____

_____

_____

_____

_____

_____

_____

_____

_____

_____

_____

_____

_____

RECIPE _____

FROM THE KITCHEN OF _____

SERVES _____

_____
_____
_____
_____
_____
_____
_____
_____
_____
_____
_____
_____
_____
_____
_____
_____
_____
_____
_____
_____
_____
_____

RECIPE _____

FROM THE KITCHEN OF _____

SERVES_____

_____

_____

_____

_____

_____

_____

_____

_____

_____

_____

_____

_____

_____

_____

_____

_____

_____

_____

_____

_____

_____

RECIPE _____

FROM THE KITCHEN OF _____

SERVES _____

RECIPE _____

FROM THE KITCHEN OF _____

                                        SERVES _____

_____

_____

_____

_____

_____

_____

_____

_____

_____

_____

_____

_____

_____

_____

_____

_____

_____

_____

_____

_____

_____

RECIPE _____

FROM THE KITCHEN OF _____

SERVES _____

_____
_____
_____
_____
_____
_____
_____
_____
_____
_____
_____
_____
_____
_____
_____
_____
_____
_____
_____
_____
_____
_____
_____

RECIPE _____

FROM THE KITCHEN OF _____

SERVES _____

_____
_____
_____
_____
_____
_____
_____
_____
_____
_____
_____
_____
_____
_____
_____
_____
_____
_____
_____
_____
_____
_____
_____

RECIPE _____

FROM THE KITCHEN OF _____

                                 SERVES _____

RECIPE _____

FROM THE KITCHEN OF _____

SERVES _____

_____

_____

_____

_____

_____

_____

_____

_____

_____

_____

_____

_____

_____

_____

_____

_____

_____

_____

_____

_____

_____

_____

_____

RECIPE _____

FROM THE KITCHEN OF _____

                                    SERVES _____

_____
_____
_____
_____
_____
_____
_____
_____
_____
_____
_____
_____
_____
_____
_____
_____
_____
_____
_____
_____
_____
_____

RECIPE _____

FROM THE KITCHEN OF _____

                                            SERVES _____

_____

_____

_____

_____

_____

_____

_____

_____

_____

_____

_____

_____

_____

_____

_____

_____

_____

_____

_____

_____

_____

_____

_____

RECIPE _____

FROM THE KITCHEN OF _____

SERVES _____

_____

_____

_____

_____

_____

_____

_____

_____

_____

_____

_____

_____

_____

_____

_____

_____

_____

_____

_____

_____

_____

_____

RECIPE _____

FROM THE KITCHEN OF _____

                              SERVES _____

_____

_____

_____

_____

_____

_____

_____

_____

_____

_____

_____

_____

_____

_____

_____

_____

_____

_____

_____

_____

_____

RECIPE _____

FROM THE KITCHEN OF _____

SERVES _____

_____

_____

_____

_____

_____

_____

_____

_____

_____

_____

_____

_____

_____

_____

_____

_____

_____

_____

_____

_____

RECIPE _____

FROM THE KITCHEN OF _____

                              SERVES _____

_____
_____
_____
_____
_____
_____
_____
_____
_____
_____
_____
_____
_____
_____
_____
_____
_____
_____
_____
_____
_____
_____
_____
_____

RECIPE _____

FROM THE KITCHEN OF _____

                                            SERVES _____

_____

_____

_____

_____

_____

_____

_____

_____

_____

_____

_____

_____

_____

_____

_____

_____

_____

_____

_____

_____

_____

_____

RECIPE _____

FROM THE KITCHEN OF _____

SERVES _____

_____

_____

_____

_____

_____

_____

_____

_____

_____

_____

_____

_____

_____

_____

_____

_____

_____

_____

_____

_____

_____

_____

RECIPE _____

FROM THE KITCHEN OF _____

                              SERVES _____

_____
_____
_____
_____
_____
_____
_____
_____
_____
_____
_____
_____
_____
_____
_____
_____
_____
_____
_____
_____
_____
_____
_____

More Recipes to Love

Use this page to organize additional recipes you want to include
in this section. List the recipe's title, source, and page number.

RECIPE TITLE	SOURCE	PAGE NUMBER

Soups & Salads

Notes

RECIPE _____

FROM THE KITCHEN OF _____

SERVES_____

_____

_____

_____

_____

_____

_____

_____

_____

_____

_____

_____

_____

_____

_____

_____

_____

_____

_____

_____

_____

_____

_____

RECIPE _____

FROM THE KITCHEN OF _____

SERVES _____

_____
_____
_____
_____
_____
_____
_____
_____
_____
_____
_____
_____
_____
_____
_____
_____
_____
_____
_____
_____
_____
_____
_____
_____

RECIPE _____

FROM THE KITCHEN OF _____

SERVES _____

_____

_____

_____

_____

_____

_____

_____

_____

_____

_____

_____

_____

_____

_____

_____

_____

_____

_____

_____

_____

RECIPE _____

FROM THE KITCHEN OF _____

                                        SERVES _____

_____

_____

_____

_____

_____

_____

_____

_____

_____

_____

_____

_____

_____

_____

_____

_____

_____

_____

_____

_____

_____

_____

RECIPE _____

FROM THE KITCHEN OF _____

SERVES _____

_____
_____
_____
_____
_____
_____
_____
_____
_____
_____
_____
_____
_____
_____
_____
_____
_____
_____
_____
_____
_____
_____

RECIPE _____

FROM THE KITCHEN OF _____

                                     SERVES _____

RECIPE _____

FROM THE KITCHEN OF _____

SERVES _____

_____
_____
_____
_____
_____
_____
_____
_____
_____
_____
_____
_____
_____
_____
_____
_____
_____
_____
_____
_____
_____
_____
_____
_____
_____
_____

RECIPE _____

FROM THE KITCHEN OF _____

SERVES _____

_____
_____
_____
_____
_____
_____
_____
_____
_____
_____
_____
_____
_____
_____
_____
_____
_____
_____
_____
_____
_____
_____

RECIPE _____

FROM THE KITCHEN OF _____

SERVES _____

_____

_____

_____

_____

_____

_____

_____

_____

_____

_____

_____

_____

_____

_____

_____

_____

_____

_____

_____

_____

_____

RECIPE _____

FROM THE KITCHEN OF _____

SERVES _____

_____

_____

_____

_____

_____

_____

_____

_____

_____

_____

_____

_____

_____

_____

_____

_____

_____

_____

_____

_____

_____

RECIPE _____

FROM THE KITCHEN OF _____

SERVES _____

_____
_____
_____
_____
_____
_____
_____
_____
_____
_____
_____
_____
_____
_____
_____
_____
_____
_____
_____
_____
_____
_____
_____

RECIPE _____

FROM THE KITCHEN OF _____

SERVES _____

_____
_____
_____
_____
_____
_____
_____
_____
_____
_____
_____
_____
_____
_____
_____
_____
_____
_____
_____
_____
_____
_____
_____
_____

RECIPE _____

FROM THE KITCHEN OF _____

SERVES _____

_____

_____

_____

_____

_____

_____

_____

_____

_____

_____

_____

_____

_____

_____

_____

_____

_____

_____

_____

_____

_____

RECIPE _____

FROM THE KITCHEN OF _____

SERVES _____

_____
_____
_____
_____
_____
_____
_____
_____
_____
_____
_____
_____
_____
_____
_____
_____
_____
_____
_____
_____
_____
_____
_____

RECIPE _____

FROM THE KITCHEN OF _____

SERVES _____

_____

_____

_____

_____

_____

_____

_____

_____

_____

_____

_____

_____

_____

_____

_____

_____

_____

_____

_____

_____

_____

_____

_____

RECIPE _____

FROM THE KITCHEN OF _____

SERVES _____

_____
_____
_____
_____
_____
_____
_____
_____
_____
_____
_____
_____
_____
_____
_____
_____
_____
_____
_____
_____
_____
_____
_____
_____
_____

RECIPE _____

FROM THE KITCHEN OF _____

SERVES _____

_____
_____
_____
_____
_____
_____
_____
_____
_____
_____
_____
_____
_____
_____
_____
_____
_____
_____
_____
_____
_____
_____
_____
_____

RECIPE _____

FROM THE KITCHEN OF _____

SERVES _____

_____
_____
_____
_____
_____
_____
_____
_____
_____
_____
_____
_____
_____
_____
_____
_____
_____
_____
_____
_____
_____
_____

More Recipes to Love

Use this page to organize additional recipes you want to include
in this section. List the recipe's title, source, and page number.

RECIPE TITLE	SOURCE	PAGE NUMBER

Main Dishes

Notes

RECIPE _____

FROM THE KITCHEN OF _____

                                    SERVES _____

_____

_____

_____

_____

_____

_____

_____

_____

_____

_____

_____

_____

_____

_____

_____

_____

_____

_____

_____

_____

_____

_____

_____

_____

_____

RECIPE _____

FROM THE KITCHEN OF _____

SERVES _____

_____
_____
_____
_____
_____
_____
_____
_____
_____
_____
_____
_____
_____
_____
_____
_____
_____
_____
_____
_____
_____
_____
_____

RECIPE _____

FROM THE KITCHEN OF _____

SERVES _____

RECIPE _____

FROM THE KITCHEN OF _____

                                             SERVES _____

RECIPE _____

FROM THE KITCHEN OF _____

SERVES _____

_____

_____

_____

_____

_____

_____

_____

_____

_____

_____

_____

_____

_____

_____

_____

_____

_____

_____

_____

_____

_____

RECIPE _____

FROM THE KITCHEN OF _____

                                    SERVES _____

_____
_____
_____
_____
_____
_____
_____
_____
_____
_____
_____
_____
_____
_____
_____
_____
_____
_____
_____
_____
_____
_____
_____
_____

RECIPE _____

FROM THE KITCHEN OF _____

SERVES _____

_____
_____
_____
_____
_____
_____
_____
_____
_____
_____
_____
_____
_____
_____
_____
_____
_____
_____
_____
_____
_____
_____
_____
_____

RECIPE _____

FROM THE KITCHEN OF _____

SERVES _____

_____

_____

_____

_____

_____

_____

_____

_____

_____

_____

_____

_____

_____

_____

_____

_____

_____

_____

_____

_____

_____

_____

RECIPE _____

FROM THE KITCHEN OF _____

SERVES _____

_____

_____

_____

_____

_____

_____

_____

_____

_____

_____

_____

_____

_____

_____

_____

_____

_____

_____

_____

_____

_____

_____

_____

_____

RECIPE _____

FROM THE KITCHEN OF _____

                                        SERVES _____

_____

_____

_____

_____

_____

_____

_____

_____

_____

_____

_____

_____

_____

_____

_____

_____

_____

_____

_____

_____

_____

RECIPE _____

FROM THE KITCHEN OF _____

                                                SERVES _____

RECIPE _____

FROM THE KITCHEN OF _____

SERVES _____

_____
_____
_____
_____
_____
_____
_____
_____
_____
_____
_____
_____
_____
_____
_____
_____
_____
_____
_____
_____
_____
_____

RECIPE _____

FROM THE KITCHEN OF _____

SERVES _____

_____

_____

_____

_____

_____

_____

_____

_____

_____

_____

_____

_____

_____

_____

_____

_____

_____

_____

_____

_____

_____

RECIPE _____

FROM THE KITCHEN OF _____

SERVES _____

_____
_____
_____
_____
_____
_____
_____
_____
_____
_____
_____
_____
_____
_____
_____
_____
_____
_____
_____
_____
_____
_____
_____

RECIPE _____

FROM THE KITCHEN OF _____

SERVES _____

_____

_____

_____

_____

_____

_____

_____

_____

_____

_____

_____

_____

_____

_____

_____

_____

_____

_____

_____

_____

_____

_____

_____

_____

RECIPE _____

FROM THE KITCHEN OF _____

                                    SERVES _____

_____
_____
_____
_____
_____
_____
_____
_____
_____
_____
_____
_____
_____
_____
_____
_____
_____
_____
_____
_____
_____
_____
_____
_____

RECIPE _____

FROM THE KITCHEN OF _____

SERVES _____

_____

_____

_____

_____

_____

_____

_____

_____

_____

_____

_____

_____

_____

_____

_____

_____

_____

_____

_____

_____

_____

_____

RECIPE _____

FROM THE KITCHEN OF _____

SERVES _____

_____
_____
_____
_____
_____
_____
_____
_____
_____
_____
_____
_____
_____
_____
_____
_____
_____
_____
_____
_____
_____
_____
_____
_____

More Recipes to Love

Use this page to organize additional recipes you want to include
in this section. List the recipe's title, source, and page number.

RECIPE TITLE	SOURCE	PAGE NUMBER

Side Dishes

Notes

RECIPE _____

FROM THE KITCHEN OF _____

SERVES _____

_____

_____

_____

_____

_____

_____

_____

_____

_____

_____

_____

_____

_____

_____

_____

_____

_____

_____

_____

_____

_____

_____

RECIPE _____

FROM THE KITCHEN OF _____

SERVES _____

_____
_____
_____
_____
_____
_____
_____
_____
_____
_____
_____
_____
_____
_____
_____
_____
_____
_____
_____
_____
_____
_____
_____

RECIPE _____

FROM THE KITCHEN OF _____

SERVES _____

_____
_____
_____
_____
_____
_____
_____
_____
_____
_____
_____
_____
_____
_____
_____
_____
_____
_____
_____
_____
_____
_____
_____

RECIPE _____

FROM THE KITCHEN OF _____

SERVES _____

_____
_____
_____
_____
_____
_____
_____
_____
_____
_____
_____
_____
_____
_____
_____
_____
_____
_____
_____
_____
_____
_____

RECIPE _____

FROM THE KITCHEN OF _____

SERVES _____

_____

_____

_____

_____

_____

_____

_____

_____

_____

_____

_____

_____

_____

_____

_____

_____

_____

_____

_____

_____

_____

_____

_____

RECIPE _____

FROM THE KITCHEN OF _____

SERVES _____

_____
_____
_____
_____
_____
_____
_____
_____
_____
_____
_____
_____
_____
_____
_____
_____
_____
_____
_____
_____
_____
_____
_____

RECIPE _____

FROM THE KITCHEN OF _____

SERVES _____

_____

_____

_____

_____

_____

_____

_____

_____

_____

_____

_____

_____

_____

_____

_____

_____

_____

_____

_____

_____

_____

_____

_____

RECIPE _____

FROM THE KITCHEN OF _____

SERVES _____

_____
_____
_____
_____
_____
_____
_____
_____
_____
_____
_____
_____
_____
_____
_____
_____
_____
_____
_____
_____
_____
_____
_____
_____

RECIPE _____

FROM THE KITCHEN OF _____

SERVES _____

_____
_____
_____
_____
_____
_____
_____
_____
_____
_____
_____
_____
_____
_____
_____
_____
_____
_____
_____
_____
_____

RECIPE _____

FROM THE KITCHEN OF _____

SERVES _____

_____

_____

_____

_____

_____

_____

_____

_____

_____

_____

_____

_____

_____

_____

_____

_____

_____

_____

_____

_____

_____

RECIPE _____

FROM THE KITCHEN OF _____

SERVES _____

_____

_____

_____

_____

_____

_____

_____

_____

_____

_____

_____

_____

_____

_____

_____

_____

_____

_____

_____

_____

_____

_____

_____

RECIPE _____

FROM THE KITCHEN OF _____

SERVES _____

_____
_____
_____
_____
_____
_____
_____
_____
_____
_____
_____
_____
_____
_____
_____
_____
_____
_____
_____
_____
_____
_____
_____

RECIPE _____

FROM THE KITCHEN OF _____

SERVES _____

_____

_____

_____

_____

_____

_____

_____

_____

_____

_____

_____

_____

_____

_____

_____

_____

_____

_____

_____

_____

_____

RECIPE _____

FROM THE KITCHEN OF _____

SERVES _____

_____

_____

_____

_____

_____

_____

_____

_____

_____

_____

_____

_____

_____

_____

_____

_____

_____

_____

_____

_____

RECIPE _____

FROM THE KITCHEN OF _____

SERVES _____

_____

_____

_____

_____

_____

_____

_____

_____

_____

_____

_____

_____

_____

_____

_____

_____

_____

_____

_____

_____

_____

_____

_____

RECIPE _____

FROM THE KITCHEN OF _____

SERVES _____

_____

_____

_____

_____

_____

_____

_____

_____

_____

_____

_____

_____

_____

_____

_____

_____

_____

_____

_____

_____

_____

_____

RECIPE _____

FROM THE KITCHEN OF _____

SERVES _____

_____

_____

_____

_____

_____

_____

_____

_____

_____

_____

_____

_____

_____

_____

_____

_____

_____

_____

_____

_____

_____

_____

_____

RECIPE _____

FROM THE KITCHEN OF _____

SERVES _____

_____

_____

_____

_____

_____

_____

_____

_____

_____

_____

_____

_____

_____

_____

_____

_____

_____

_____

_____

_____

_____

_____

More Recipes to Love

Use this page to organize additional recipes you want to include in this section. List the recipe's title, source, and page number.

RECIPE TITLE	SOURCE	PAGE NUMBER

Baked Goods

Notes

RECIPE _____

FROM THE KITCHEN OF _____

SERVES _____

_____

_____

_____

_____

_____

_____

_____

_____

_____

_____

_____

_____

_____

_____

_____

_____

_____

_____

_____

_____

_____

_____

_____

_____

RECIPE _____

FROM THE KITCHEN OF _____

SERVES _____

_____
_____
_____
_____
_____
_____
_____
_____
_____
_____
_____
_____
_____
_____
_____
_____
_____
_____
_____
_____
_____
_____
_____
_____

RECIPE _____

FROM THE KITCHEN OF _____

SERVES _____

_____

_____

_____

_____

_____

_____

_____

_____

_____

_____

_____

_____

_____

_____

_____

_____

_____

_____

_____

_____

RECIPE _____

FROM THE KITCHEN OF _____

SERVES _____

_____
_____
_____
_____
_____
_____
_____
_____
_____
_____
_____
_____
_____
_____
_____
_____
_____
_____
_____
_____
_____
_____

RECIPE _____

FROM THE KITCHEN OF _____

SERVES _____

_____

_____

_____

_____

_____

_____

_____

_____

_____

_____

_____

_____

_____

_____

_____

_____

_____

_____

_____

_____

_____

_____

_____

RECIPE _____

FROM THE KITCHEN OF _____

                                    SERVES _____

_____

_____

_____

_____

_____

_____

_____

_____

_____

_____

_____

_____

_____

_____

_____

_____

_____

_____

_____

_____

RECIPE _____

FROM THE KITCHEN OF _____

SERVES _____

_____

_____

_____

_____

_____

_____

_____

_____

_____

_____

_____

_____

_____

_____

_____

_____

_____

_____

_____

_____

_____

_____

RECIPE _____

FROM THE KITCHEN OF _____

SERVES _____

_____
_____
_____
_____
_____
_____
_____
_____
_____
_____
_____
_____
_____
_____
_____
_____
_____
_____
_____
_____
_____
_____
_____

RECIPE _____

FROM THE KITCHEN OF _____

SERVES _____

_____

_____

_____

_____

_____

_____

_____

_____

_____

_____

_____

_____

_____

_____

_____

_____

_____

_____

_____

_____

_____

_____

RECIPE _____

FROM THE KITCHEN OF _____

SERVES _____

_____

_____

_____

_____

_____

_____

_____

_____

_____

_____

_____

_____

_____

_____

_____

_____

_____

_____

_____

_____

_____

_____

_____

RECIPE _____

FROM THE KITCHEN OF _____

SERVES _____

_____
_____
_____
_____
_____
_____
_____
_____
_____
_____
_____
_____
_____
_____
_____
_____
_____
_____
_____
_____
_____
_____
_____
_____

RECIPE _____

FROM THE KITCHEN OF _____

SERVES _____

_____

_____

_____

_____

_____

_____

_____

_____

_____

_____

_____

_____

_____

_____

_____

_____

_____

_____

_____

_____

_____

_____

RECIPE _____

FROM THE KITCHEN OF _____

SERVES _____

_____

_____

_____

_____

_____

_____

_____

_____

_____

_____

_____

_____

_____

_____

_____

_____

_____

_____

_____

_____

_____

_____

_____

RECIPE _____

FROM THE KITCHEN OF _____

SERVES _____

_____
_____
_____
_____
_____
_____
_____
_____
_____
_____
_____
_____
_____
_____
_____
_____
_____
_____
_____
_____
_____

RECIPE _____

FROM THE KITCHEN OF _____

SERVES _____

_____
_____
_____
_____
_____
_____
_____
_____
_____
_____
_____
_____
_____
_____
_____
_____
_____
_____
_____
_____
_____
_____

RECIPE _____

FROM THE KITCHEN OF _____

SERVES _____

_____
_____
_____
_____
_____
_____
_____
_____
_____
_____
_____
_____
_____
_____
_____
_____
_____
_____
_____
_____
_____
_____

RECIPE _____

FROM THE KITCHEN OF _____

SERVES _____

_____

_____

_____

_____

_____

_____

_____

_____

_____

_____

_____

_____

_____

_____

_____

_____

_____

_____

_____

_____

_____

_____

RECIPE _____

FROM THE KITCHEN OF _____

SERVES _____

_____
_____
_____
_____
_____
_____
_____
_____
_____
_____
_____
_____
_____
_____
_____
_____
_____
_____
_____
_____
_____
_____

More Recipes to Love

Use this page to organize additional recipes you want to include
in this section. List the recipe's title, source, and page number.

RECIPE TITLE	SOURCE	PAGE NUMBER
_____	_____	_____
_____	_____	_____
_____	_____	_____
_____	_____	_____
_____	_____	_____
_____	_____	_____
_____	_____	_____
_____	_____	_____
_____	_____	_____
_____	_____	_____
_____	_____	_____
_____	_____	_____
_____	_____	_____
_____	_____	_____
_____	_____	_____
_____	_____	_____
_____	_____	_____

Desserts

Notes

RECIPE _____

FROM THE KITCHEN OF _____

SERVES _____

_____

_____

_____

_____

_____

_____

_____

_____

_____

_____

_____

_____

_____

_____

_____

_____

_____

_____

_____

_____

_____

_____

RECIPE _____

FROM THE KITCHEN OF _____

SERVES _____

_____

_____

_____

_____

_____

_____

_____

_____

_____

_____

_____

_____

_____

_____

_____

_____

_____

_____

_____

_____

_____

_____

_____

RECIPE _____

FROM THE KITCHEN OF _____

SERVES _____

_____

_____

_____

_____

_____

_____

_____

_____

_____

_____

_____

_____

_____

_____

_____

_____

_____

_____

_____

_____

RECIPE _____

FROM THE KITCHEN OF _____

SERVES _____

_____
_____
_____
_____
_____
_____
_____
_____
_____
_____
_____
_____
_____
_____
_____
_____
_____
_____
_____
_____
_____
_____
_____

RECIPE _____

FROM THE KITCHEN OF _____

SERVES _____

_____

_____

_____

_____

_____

_____

_____

_____

_____

_____

_____

_____

_____

_____

_____

_____

_____

_____

_____

_____

RECIPE _____

FROM THE KITCHEN OF _____

SERVES _____

_____

_____

_____

_____

_____

_____

_____

_____

_____

_____

_____

_____

_____

_____

_____

_____

_____

_____

_____

_____

_____

RECIPE _____

FROM THE KITCHEN OF _____

SERVES _____

_____

_____

_____

_____

_____

_____

_____

_____

_____

_____

_____

_____

_____

_____

_____

_____

_____

_____

_____

_____

_____

_____

RECIPE _____

FROM THE KITCHEN OF _____

SERVES _____

_____
_____
_____
_____
_____
_____
_____
_____
_____
_____
_____
_____
_____
_____
_____
_____
_____
_____
_____
_____
_____
_____
_____
_____
_____

RECIPE _____

FROM THE KITCHEN OF _____

SERVES _____

_____

_____

_____

_____

_____

_____

_____

_____

_____

_____

_____

_____

_____

_____

_____

_____

_____

_____

_____

_____

_____

RECIPE _____

FROM THE KITCHEN OF _____

SERVES _____

_____

_____

_____

_____

_____

_____

_____

_____

_____

_____

_____

_____

_____

_____

_____

_____

_____

_____

_____

_____

RECIPE _____

FROM THE KITCHEN OF _____

SERVES _____

_____
_____
_____
_____
_____
_____
_____
_____
_____
_____
_____
_____
_____
_____
_____
_____
_____
_____
_____
_____
_____
_____
_____

RECIPE _____

FROM THE KITCHEN OF _____

SERVES _____

_____
_____
_____
_____
_____
_____
_____
_____
_____
_____
_____
_____
_____
_____
_____
_____
_____
_____
_____
_____
_____
_____
_____
_____
_____

RECIPE _____

FROM THE KITCHEN OF _____

SERVES _____

_____

_____

_____

_____

_____

_____

_____

_____

_____

_____

_____

_____

_____

_____

_____

_____

_____

_____

_____

_____

_____

RECIPE _____

FROM THE KITCHEN OF _____

SERVES _____

_____
_____
_____
_____
_____
_____
_____
_____
_____
_____
_____
_____
_____
_____
_____
_____
_____
_____
_____
_____
_____
_____
_____
_____

RECIPE _____

FROM THE KITCHEN OF _____

SERVES _____

_____
_____
_____
_____
_____
_____
_____
_____
_____
_____
_____
_____
_____
_____
_____
_____
_____
_____
_____
_____

RECIPE _____

FROM THE KITCHEN OF _____

SERVES _____

_____
_____
_____
_____
_____
_____
_____
_____
_____
_____
_____
_____
_____
_____
_____
_____
_____
_____
_____
_____
_____
_____
_____
_____

RECIPE _____

FROM THE KITCHEN OF _____

SERVES _____

_____

_____

_____

_____

_____

_____

_____

_____

_____

_____

_____

_____

_____

_____

_____

_____

_____

_____

_____

_____

RECIPE _____

FROM THE KITCHEN OF _____

SERVES _____

_____
_____
_____
_____
_____
_____
_____
_____
_____
_____
_____
_____
_____
_____
_____
_____
_____
_____
_____
_____

More Recipes to Love

Use this page to organize additional recipes you want to include
in this section. List the recipe's title, source, and page number.

RECIPE TITLE	SOURCE	PAGE NUMBER

Holiday Dishes

Notes

RECIPE _____

FROM THE KITCHEN OF _____

SERVES _____

_____

_____

_____

_____

_____

_____

_____

_____

_____

_____

_____

_____

_____

_____

_____

_____

_____

_____

_____

_____

_____

_____

_____

RECIPE _____

FROM THE KITCHEN OF _____

SERVES _____

_____

_____

_____

_____

_____

_____

_____

_____

_____

_____

_____

_____

_____

_____

_____

_____

_____

_____

_____

_____

_____

_____

_____

_____

_____

_____

_____

RECIPE _____

FROM THE KITCHEN OF _____

SERVES _____

_____

_____

_____

_____

_____

_____

_____

_____

_____

_____

_____

_____

_____

_____

_____

_____

_____

_____

_____

_____

_____

RECIPE _____

FROM THE KITCHEN OF _____

SERVES _____

_____

_____

_____

_____

_____

_____

_____

_____

_____

_____

_____

_____

_____

_____

_____

_____

_____

_____

_____

_____

_____

_____

_____

RECIPE _____

FROM THE KITCHEN OF _____

SERVES _____

_____
_____
_____
_____
_____
_____
_____
_____
_____
_____
_____
_____
_____
_____
_____
_____
_____
_____
_____
_____
_____
_____
_____

RECIPE _____

FROM THE KITCHEN OF _____

SERVES _____

_____
_____
_____
_____
_____
_____
_____
_____
_____
_____
_____
_____
_____
_____
_____
_____
_____
_____
_____
_____
_____
_____
_____
_____
_____

RECIPE _____

FROM THE KITCHEN OF _____

                                                SERVES _____

_____
_____
_____
_____
_____
_____
_____
_____
_____
_____
_____
_____
_____
_____
_____
_____
_____
_____
_____
_____
_____
_____

RECIPE _____

FROM THE KITCHEN OF _____

SERVES _____

_____
_____
_____
_____
_____
_____
_____
_____
_____
_____
_____
_____
_____
_____
_____
_____
_____
_____
_____
_____
_____
_____
_____

RECIPE _____

FROM THE KITCHEN OF _____

SERVES _____

_____
_____
_____
_____
_____
_____
_____
_____
_____
_____
_____
_____
_____
_____
_____
_____
_____
_____
_____
_____
_____
_____

RECIPE _____

FROM THE KITCHEN OF _____

SERVES _____

_____
_____
_____
_____
_____
_____
_____
_____
_____
_____
_____
_____
_____
_____
_____
_____
_____
_____
_____
_____
_____
_____
_____
_____
_____

RECIPE _____

FROM THE KITCHEN OF _____

SERVES _____

_____

_____

_____

_____

_____

_____

_____

_____

_____

_____

_____

_____

_____

_____

_____

_____

_____

_____

_____

_____

_____

_____

RECIPE _____

FROM THE KITCHEN OF _____

SERVES _____

_____

_____

_____

_____

_____

_____

_____

_____

_____

_____

_____

_____

_____

_____

_____

_____

_____

_____

_____

RECIPE _____

FROM THE KITCHEN OF _____

                                    SERVES _____

_____

_____

_____

_____

_____

_____

_____

_____

_____

_____

_____

_____

_____

_____

_____

_____

_____

_____

_____

_____

_____

_____

_____

RECIPE _____

FROM THE KITCHEN OF _____

SERVES _____

_____
_____
_____
_____
_____
_____
_____
_____
_____
_____
_____
_____
_____
_____
_____
_____
_____
_____
_____
_____
_____
_____
_____
_____
_____

RECIPE _____

FROM THE KITCHEN OF _____

SERVES _____

_____
_____
_____
_____
_____
_____
_____
_____
_____
_____
_____
_____
_____
_____
_____
_____
_____
_____
_____
_____
_____
_____
_____
_____
_____
_____

RECIPE _____

FROM THE KITCHEN OF _____

SERVES _____

_____

_____

_____

_____

_____

_____

_____

_____

_____

_____

_____

_____

_____

_____

_____

_____

_____

_____

_____

_____

_____

_____

RECIPE _____

FROM THE KITCHEN OF _____

SERVES _____

_____

_____

_____

_____

_____

_____

_____

_____

_____

_____

_____

_____

_____

_____

_____

_____

_____

_____

_____

_____

_____

RECIPE _____

FROM THE KITCHEN OF _____

                                        SERVES _____

More Recipes to Love

Use this page to organize additional recipes you want to include
in this section. List the recipe's title, source, and page number.

RECIPE TITLE	SOURCE	PAGE NUMBER